Samba
Pocket Reference

Robert Eckstein,
David Collier-Brown,
and Peter Kelly

O'REILLY®

Beijing • Cambridge • Farnham • Köln • Paris • Sebastopol • Taipei • Tokyo

Samba Pocket Reference

by Robert Eckstein, David Collier-Brown, and Peter Kelly

Published by O'Reilly & Associates, Inc., 101 Morris Street, Sebastopol, CA 95472.

Editor: Andy Oram

Production Editors: Linley Dolby and Claire Cloutier

Cover Designer: Ellie Volckhausen

Printing History:

April 2001:   First Edition

0-596-00099-5

[C]

Table of Contents

Samba Pocket Reference

Introduction

Samba is a suite of Unix applications that speak the Server Message Block (SMB) protocol. Many operating systems, including Windows and OS/2, use SMB to perform client/server networking. By supporting this protocol, Samba allows Unix servers to get in on the action, communicating with the same networking protocol as Microsoft Windows products. This book covers Version 2.0 of Samba, and many 2.2 options, but points out which options have been recently added in case you are still running an earlier version.

This pocket reference is aimed at system administrators who have already learned the basics of Samba and related information about Windows clients and domains. If you are new to Samba, we recommend you read *Using Samba*, by Robert Eckstein, David Collier-Brown, and Peter Kelly (O'Reilly). The material in this book comes from two appendixes of *Using Samba*.

A Samba-enabled Unix machine can masquerade as a server on your Microsoft network and offer the following services:

- Sharing one or more filesystems

- Sharing printers installed on both the server and its clients

- Assisting clients with Network Neighborhood browsing

- Authenticating clients logging onto a Windows domain

- Providing or assisting with WINS nameserver resolution

Contents

"Configuration File Options" lists the types of lines you can put in your Samba configuration file, usually named *smb.conf.*

"Samba Daemons" lists command-line options and related information for running the Samba daemons, and "Samba Distribution Programs" lists various commands included in the Samba distribution that you can run from the Unix shell on the system hosting Samba.

The Samba daemons are:

smbd
> A program responsible for managing the shared resources between the Samba server machine and its clients. It provides file, print, and browser services to SMB clients across one or more networks. *smbd* handles all notifications between the Samba server and the network clients. In addition, it is responsible for user authentication, resource locking, and data sharing through the SMB protocol.

nmbd
> A simple nameserver that mimics the WINS and NetBIOS nameserver functionality, as you might expect to encounter with the LAN Manager package. This daemon listens for nameserver requests and provides the appropriate information when called upon. It also provides browse lists for the Network Neighborhood, and participates in browsing elections.

The Samba commands are:

nmblookup
> A program that provides NetBIOS over TCP/IP name lookups

rpcclient
> A Samba developer's tool that exercises the remote procedure call (RPC) interfaces of an SMB server

---

smbclient
> An FTP-like Unix client that can be used to connect to Samba shares

smbpasswd
> A program that allows an administrator to change the encrypted passwords used by Samba

smbsh
> A shell that allows users to access files and directories on a remote Windows share as if the share were a regular Unix directory; available if Samba is compiled with the --with-smbwrappers option

smbstatus
> A program for reporting the current network connections to the shares on a Samba server

smbtar
> A program for backing up data in shares, similar to the Unix *tar* command

tcpdump
> A version of the traditional Unix packet-tracing program that has been enhanced to understand the SMB protocol

testparm
> A simple program to validate the Samba configuration file

testprns
> A program that tests whether various printers are recognized by the *smbd* daemon

Font Conventions

The following font conventions are followed throughout this book:

Italic
> Used for filenames, file extensions, URLs, executable files, commands, Samba daemons, and emphasis

---

Constant width
> Used to indicate Samba configuration options, code that appears in the text, variables, and command-line information that should be typed verbatim on the screen

Constant width bold
> Used for commands that are entered by the user, and new configuration options that we wish to bring to readers' attention

Constant width italic
> Used to indicate replaceable content in code and command-line information

[]
> Used to indicate optional elements in code

Configuration File Options

This section lists each of the options that can be used in a Samba configuration file, which is usually named *smb.conf.* Most configuration files contain a global section of options that apply to all directories (shares), and a separate section for various individual shares. If an option applies only to the global section, [global] appears before its name in the following reference section. Any lists mentioned are space-separated, except where noted. A glossary of terms and a list of variables Samba recognizes follow this reference section.

[global] add user script = script
allowable values: full path to shell script
default: NULL

Specifies a script that creates a new user on the system hosting the Samba server. This script runs as root when access to a Samba share is attempted by a Windows user who does not have an account on the hosting system, but does have an account maintained by a primary domain controller on a different system. The script should accept the name of the user as a single argument, which matches the behavior of typical *adduser* scripts. Samba honors the %u value (username) as the argument to the script. Requires security = server or security = domain. See also delete user script.

---

admin users = user list
allowable values: user list
default: NULL

Specifies a list of users who will be granted root permissions on the share by Samba.

allow hosts = host list
allowable values: list of hosts or networks
default: NULL

Specifies a list of machines that may connect to a share or shares. If NULL, any machine can access the share unless there is a hosts deny option. Synonym for hosts allow.

[global] allow trusted domains = boolean
allowable values: YES, NO
default: YES

Allows access to users who lack accounts on the Samba server but have accounts in another, trusted domain. Requires security = server or security = domain.

[global] announce as = system type
allowable values: NT, Win95, WfW
default: NT

Has Samba announce itself as something other than an NT server. Discouraged because it interferes with serving browse lists.

[global] announce version = number.number
allowable values: any
default: 4.2

Instructs Samba to announce itself as a different version SMB server. Discouraged.

[global] auto services = share list
allowable values: list of shares
default: NULL

Specifies a list of shares that will always appear in browse lists. Also called preload.

available = boolean
allowable values: YES, NO
default: YES

If set to NO, denies access to a share. Doesn't affect browsing.

[global] bind interfaces only = boolean
allowable values: YES, NO
default: NO

If set to YES, shares and browsing will be provided only on interfaces in an interfaces list (see `interfaces`). If you set this option to YES, be sure to add 127.0.0.1 to the interfaces list to allow *smbpasswd* to connect to the local machine to change passwords. This is a convenience option; it does not improve security.

---

blocking locks = boolean
allowable values: YES, NO
default: YES

If YES, honors byte range lock requests with time limits. Samba will queue the requests and retry them until the time period expires.

---

browsable = boolean
allowable values: YES, NO
default: YES

Allows a share to be announced in browse lists. Also called `browseable`.

[global] browse list = boolean
allowable values: YES, NO
default: YES

Turns on `browse list` from this server. Avoid changing.

[global] case sensitive = boolean
allowable values: YES, NO
default: NO

If YES, uses the exact case the client supplied when trying to resolve a filename. If NO, matches either upper- or lowercase name. Avoid changing. Also called `casesignames`.

[global] casesignames = boolean
allowable values: YES, NO
default: NO

Synonym for case sensitive.

[global] change notify timeout = number
allowable values: positive number
default: 60

Sets the number of seconds between checks when a client asks for notification of changes in a directory. Introduced in Samba 2.0 to limit the performance cost of the checks. Avoid lowering.

character set = name
allowable values: ISO8859-1, ISO8859-2, ISO8859-5, KOI8-R
default: NULL

If set, translates from DOS code pages to the Western European (ISO8859-1), Eastern European (ISO8859-2), Russian Cyrillic (ISO8859-5), or Alternate Russian (KOI8-R) character set. The client code page option must be set to 850.

client code page = name
allowable values: see Table 1
default: 437 (U.S. MS-DOS)

Sets the DOS code page explicitly, overriding any previous valid chars settings. Examples of values are 850 for Western European, 437 for the U.S. standard, and 932 for Japanese Shift-JIS.

Table 1. Valid Code Pages

Code Page	Definition
437	MS-DOS Latin (United States)
737	Windows 95 Greek
850	MS-DOS Latin 1 (Western European)
852	MS-DOS Latin 2 (Eastern European)
861	MS-DOS Icelandic
866	MS-DOS Cyrillic (Russian)
932	MS-DOS Japanese Shift-JIS
936	MS-DOS Simplified Chinese
949	MS-DOS Korean Hangul
950	MS-DOS Traditional Chinese

[global] code page directory = pathname
allowable values: full directory name
default: /usr/local/samba/lib/codepages

Specifies the directory that stores code pages. New in Samba 2.2.

coding system = code
allowable values: euc, cap, hex, hexN, sjis, j8bb, j8bj, jis8, j8bh, j8@b, j8@j, j8@h, j7bb, j7bj, jis7, j7bh, j7@b, j7@j, j7@h, jubb, jubj, junet, jubh, ju@b, ju@j, ju@h
default: NULL

Sets the coding system used, notably for Kanji. This is employed for filenames and should correspond to the code page in use. The client code page option must be set to 932 (Japanese Shift-JIS).

comment = text
allowable values: a text string or NULL
default: NULL

Sets the comment that appears beside a share in a NET VIEW or in the details list of a Microsoft directory window. See also the server string configuration option.

[global] config file = pathname
allowable values: full Unix pathname
default: NULL

Selects an additional Samba configuration file to read instead of the current one. Used to relocate the configuration file, or used with % variables to select custom configuration files for some users or machines.

copy = section name
allowable values: existing section's name
default: NULL

Copies the configuration of a previously seen share into the share in which this option appears. Used with % variables to select custom configurations for machines, architectures, and users. The copied section must occur earlier in the configuration file. Each option specified or copied takes precedence over earlier specifications of the option.

create mask = octal permission bits
allowable values: octal value from 0 to 0777
default: 0744

Sets the maximum allowable permissions for new files (e.g., 0755). See also directory mask. To require certain permissions to be set, see force create mask and force directory mask. Also called create mode.

create mode = octal permission bits
allowable values: octal value from 0 to 0777
default: 0744

Synonym for create mask.

[global] deadtime = number
allowable values: number of minutes
default: 0

Specifies the time in minutes before an unused connection will be terminated. Zero means never. Used to keep clients from tying up server resources for long periods of time. If used, clients will have to auto-reconnect after the specified period of inactivity. See also keepalive.

[global] debug hires timestamp = boolean
allowable values: YES, NO
default: NO

Changes the timestamps in log entries from seconds to microseconds. Useful for measuring performance. New in Samba 2.0.6.

[global] debug level = number
allowable values: number
default: 0

Sets the logging level used. Values of 3 or more slow Samba noticeably. Also called log level. Recommended value is 1.

[global] debug pid = boolean
allowable values: YES, NO
default: NO

Adds the process ID of the Samba server to log lines, to make it easier to debug a particular server. New in Samba 2.0.6.

[global] debug timestamp = boolean
allowable values: YES, NO
default: YES

Timestamps all log messages. Can be turned off when it's not useful (e.g., in debugging). Also called `timestamp logs`.

[global] debug uid = boolean
allowable values: YES, NO
default: NO

Adds the real and effective user ID and group ID of the user being served to the logs, to make it easier to debug one particular user. New in Samba 2.0.6.

[global] default = share name
allowable values: share name
default: NULL

Specifies the name of a service (share) to provide if someone requests a service he doesn't have permission to use or that doesn't exist. As of Samba 1.9.14, the path will be set from the name the client specified, with any "_" characters changed to "/" characters, allowing access to any directory on the Samba server. Use is strongly discouraged. Also called `default service`.

default case = case
allowable values: LOWER, UPPER
default: LOWER

Sets the case in which to store new filenames. LOWER indicates lowercase, and UPPER indicates uppercase.

[global] default service = share name
allowable values: share name
default: NULL

Synonym for `default`.

delete readonly = boolean
allowable values: NO, YES
default: NO

If set to YES, allows delete requests to remove read-only files. This is not allowed in DOS/Windows but is normal in Unix, which has separate directory permissions. Used with programs such as RCS.

[global] delete user script = command
allowable values: full path to script
default: NULL

Runs this script as root when a user connects who no longer has an account on the domain's PDC. Honors %u. Can be used to delete the user account automatically from the Samba server's host. Requires security = domain. Use with caution. See also add user script.

delete veto files = boolean
allowable values: NO, YES
default: NO

If set to YES, allows delete requests for a directory containing files or subdirectories the user can't see due to the veto files option. If set to NO, the directory will not be deleted and will still contain invisible files.

deny hosts = host list
allowable values: list of hosts or networks
default: NULL

Specifies a list of machines from which to refuse connections or shares. Also called hosts deny.

[global] dfree command = command
allowable values: shell command
default: varies

Specifies a command to run on the server to return free disk space. Not needed unless the OS command does not work properly.

directory = pathname
allowable values: full Unix pathname
default: varies

Sets the path to the directory provided by a file share or used by a printer share. If the option is omitted, set automatically in the [homes] share to the user's home directory; otherwise defaults to */tmp*. Honors the %u (user) and %m (machine) variables. Synonym for path.

directory mask = octal permission bits
allowable values: octal value from 0 to 0777
default: 0755

Sets the maximum allowable permissions for newly created directories. To require that certain permissions be set, see the force create mask and force directory mask options. Also called directory mode.

directory mode = octal permission bits
allowable values: octal value from 0 to 0777
default: 0755

Synonym for directory mask.

directory security mask = octal permission bits
allowable values: octal value from 0 to 0777
default: same as directory mode

Controls which permission bits can be changed if a user edits the Unix permissions of directories on the Samba server from a Windows system. Any bit that is set in the mask can be changed by the user; any bit that is clear will remain the same on the directory even if the user tries to change it. Requires nt acl support = YES. New in Version 2.0.4.

[global] dns proxy = boolean
allowable values: YES, NO
default: YES

If set to YES, and if wins server = YES, looks up hostnames in DNS when they are not found using WINS.

[global] domain logons = boolean
allowable values: YES, NO
default: NO

Allows Windows 95/98 or NT clients to store logon profiles on the Samba server. See also logon drive, logon home, logon path.

[global] domain master = boolean
allowable values: YES, NO
default: NO

Makes the server become a domain master browse-list collector, if possible, for the entire workgroup/domain.

---

dont descend = comma-separated list
allowable values: comma-separated list of paths
default: NULL

Prohibits a change directory or search in the directories specified. This is a browsing convenience option; it doesn't provide any extra security.

dos filetime resolution = boolean
allowable values: YES, NO
default: NO

Sets file times on Unix to match DOS standards (rounding to the next even second). Recommended if using Visual C++ or a PC *make* program to avoid remaking the programs unnecessarily. Use with the dos filetimes option.

dos filetimes = boolean
allowable values: YES, NO
default: NO

Allows nonowners to change file times if they can write to the files. See also dos filetime resolution.

[global] encrypt passwords = boolean
allowable values: YES, NO
default: NO

Uses Windows NT–style password encryption. Requires an *smbpasswd* file on the Samba server.

exec = command
allowable values: full path to shell command
default: NULL

Sets a command to run as the user before connecting to the share. Synonym for preexec. See also the postexec, root preexec, and root postexec options.

fake directory create times = boolean
allowable values: YES, NO
default: NO

A bug fix for users of Microsoft *nmake*. If YES, Samba sets directory create times such that *nmake* won't remake all files every time.

fake oplocks = boolean

allowable values: YES, NO

default: NO

If set, returns YES whenever a client asks if it can lock a file and cache it locally, but does not enforce the lock on the server. Use only for read-only disks, as Samba now supports real oplocks and has per-file overrides. See also oplocks and veto oplock files.

follow symlinks = boolean

allowable values: YES, NO

default: YES

If set to YES, Samba follows symlinks in a file share or shares. See the wide links option if you want to restrict symlinks to just the current share.

force create mask = octal permission bits

allowable values: octal value from 0 to 0777

default: 0

Takes effect when a user on a Windows system creates a file that resides on the Samba server. This option ensures that bits will always be set on a file when they are set in this mask. Used with the create mask configuration option. Also called force create mode.

force create mode = octal permission bits

allowable values: octal value from 0 to 0777

default: 0

Synonym for force create mask.

force directory mask = octal permission bits

allowable values: octal value from 0 to 0777

default: 0

Takes effect when a user on a Windows system creates a directory on the Samba server. This option ensures that bits will always be set on a directory when they are set in this mask. Used with directory mask. Also called force directory mode.

force directory mode = octal permission bits

allowable values: octal value from 0 to 0777

default: 0

Synonym for force directory mask.

---

force directory security mode = octal permission bits

allowable values: octal value from 0 to 0777
default: same as force directory mode

Takes effect when a user edits the Unix permissions of directories on the Samba server while the user is on a Windows system. This option ensures that bits will always be set on a directory when they are set in this mask. Requires nt acl support = YES. New in Version 2.0.4.

force group = unix group

allowable values: group
default: NULL

Sets the effective group name assigned to all users accessing a share. Used to override a user's normal groups.

force security mode = octal permission bits

allowable values: octal value from 0 to 0777
default: same as force create mode

Takes effect when a user edits the Unix permissions of files on the Samba server while the user is on a Windows system. This option ensures that bits will always be set on a file when they are set in this mask. Requires nt acl support = YES. New in Version 2.0.4.

force user = username

allowable values: username
default: NULL

Sets the effective username assigned to all users accessing a share. Discouraged.

fstype = string

allowable values: NTFS, FAT, Samba
default: NTFS

Sets the filesystem type reported to the client. Avoid changing.

[global] getwd cache = boolean

allowable values: YES, NO
default: NO

Caches the current directory for performance. Recommended with the wide links option.

group = group
allowable values: Unix group
default: NULL

An obsolete form of force group. Avoid using.

guest account = username
allowable values: username
default: NULL

Sets the name of the unprivileged Unix account to use for tasks such as printing and for accessing shares marked with guest ok.

guest ok = boolean
allowable values: YES, NO
default: NO

If set to YES, passwords are not needed for this share. Synonym for public.

guest only = boolean
allowable values: YES, NO
default: NO

Forces users of a share to log in as the guest account. Requires guest ok or public to be YES. Also called only guest.

hide dot files = boolean
allowable values: YES, NO
default: YES

Treats files beginning with a dot in a share as if they had the DOS/Windows hidden attribute set.

hide files = slash-separated list
allowable values: list of patterns, separated by / characters
default: NULL

Specifies a list of file or directory names on which to set the DOS hidden attribute. Names may contain ? or * pattern-characters and % variables. See also hide dot files and veto files.

[global] homedir map = NIS map name

allowable values: NIS map name
default: auto.home

Is used with `nis homedir` to locate a user's Unix home directory from Sun NIS (not NIS+).

hosts allow = host list

allowable values: list of hosts or networks
default: NULL

Specifies a list of machines that can access a share or shares. If NULL, any machine can access the share unless there is a `hosts deny` option. Synonym for `allow hosts`.

hosts deny = host list

allowable values: list of hosts or networks
default: NULL

Specifies a list of machines that cannot connect to a share or shares. Synonym for `deny hosts`.

[global] hosts equiv = pathname

allowable values: full Unix pathname
default: NULL

Specifies the path to a file of trusted machines from which passwordless logins are allowed. Strongly discouraged because Windows NT users can always override the username, the only security in this scheme.

include = pathname

allowable values: full Unix pathname
default: NULL

Includes the named file in *smb.conf* at the line where it appears. This option does not understand the variables %u (user), %P (current share's root directory), or %S (current share's name), because they are not set at the time the file is read.

inherit permissions = boolean

allowable values: YES, NO

default: NO

If set, files and subdirectories will be created with the same permissions as their parent directories. This allows Unix directory permissions to be propagated automatically to new files and subdirectories, especially in the [homes] share. This option overrides create mask, directory mask, force create mode, and force directory mode, but not map archive, map hidden, or map system. Samba never sets the setuid bit when creating a file or directory. This option is new in 2.0.7.

[global] interfaces = interface list

allowable values: IP addresses separated by spaces

default: NULL

Sets the interfaces to which Samba will respond. The default is the machine's primary interface only. Recommended on multihomed machines or to override erroneous addresses and netmasks.

invalid users = user list

allowable values: list of users

default: NULL

Specifies a list of users that will not be permitted access to a share or shares.

[global] keepalive = number

allowable values: number of seconds

default: 0

Sets the number of seconds between checks for a crashed client. The default of 0 causes no checks to be performed. Setting SOCKET OPTIONS=KEEPALIVE will turn on checks every four hours. A value of 3600 (every 10 minutes) is recommended if you want checks more often than every four hours. See also socket options for another approach.

[global] kernel oplocks = boolean

allowable values: YES, NO

default: automatic

Breaks the oplock when a Unix process accesses an oplocked file, preventing corruption. Set to YES on operating systems supporting this; otherwise set to NO. Avoid changing.

---

level2 oplocks = boolean
allowable values: YES, NO
default: NO in 2.0.x, YES in 2.2

Allows files to be cached read-only on the client even if multiple clients have opened the file. This allows executables to be cached locally, improving performance. Introduced in 2.0.5.

[global] lm announce = value
allowable values: AUTO, YES, NO
default: AUTO

Produces OS/2 SMB broadcasts at an interval specified by the lm interval option. YES/NO turns them on/off unconditionally. AUTO causes the Samba server to wait for a LAN manager announcement from another client before sending one out. Required for OS/2 client browsing.

[global] lm interval = number
allowable values: number of seconds
default: 60

Sets the time period, in seconds, between OS/2 SMB broadcast announcements.

[global] load printers = boolean
allowable values: YES, NO
default: YES

Loads all printer names from the system's *printcap* file into the browse list. Uses configuration options from the [printers] section.

[global] local master = boolean
allowable values: YES, NO
default: YES

Stands for election as the local master browser. See also domain master and os level.

[global] lock directory = pathname
allowable values: full Unix pathname
default: /usr/local/samba/var/locks

Sets a directory in which to keep lock files. The directory must be writable by Samba, and readable by everyone. Also called lock dir.

locking = boolean
allowable values: YES, NO
default: YES

Performs file locking. If set to NO, Samba accepts lock requests but won't actually lock resources. Turn off for read-only filesystems.

[global] log file = pathname
allowable values: full Unix pathname
default: varies

Sets the name and location of the log file. Allows all % variables.

[global] log level = number
allowable values: number
default: 0

Sets the logging level used. Values of 3 or more slow the system noticeably. Recommended value is 1. Synonym for debug level.

[global] logon drive = drive
allowable values: DOS drive name
default: None

Sets the drive on Windows NT (only) of the logon path.

[global] logon home = path
allowable values: full Unix pathname
default: \\ %N\ %U

Sets the home directory of a Windows 95/98 or NT Workstation user. Allows NET USE H:/HOME from the command prompt.

[global] logon path = pathname
allowable values: full Windows pathname
default: \\ %N\ %U\ *profile*

Sets the path to the Windows profile directory. This contains the *USER.MAN* and/or *USER.DAT* profile files and the Windows 95 Desktop, Start Menu, Network Neighborhood, and program folders.

[global] logon script = pathname
allowable values: full Windows pathname
default: NULL

Sets the pathname relative to [netlogin] share of a DOS/NT script to run on the client at login time. Allows all % variables.

---

lppause command = command
allowable values: full path to shell command
default: varies

Sets the command to pause a print job. Honors the %p (printer name) and %j (job number) variables.

[global] lpq cache time = number
allowable values: number of seconds
default: 10

Sets how long to keep print queue (lpq) status cached, in seconds.

lpq command = command
allowable values: full path to shell command
default: varies

Sets the command used to get printer status. Usually initialized to a default value by the printing option. Honors the %p (printer name) variable.

lpresume command = command
allowable values: full path to shell command
default: varies

Sets the command to resume a paused print job. Honors the %p (printer name) and %j (job number) variables.

lprm command = command
allowable values: full path to shell command
default: varies

Sets the command to delete a print job. Usually initialized to a default value by the printing option. Honors the %p (printer name) and %j (job number) variables.

machine password timeout = number
allowable values: number of seconds
default: 604800 (1 week)

Sets the period between (NT domain) machine password changes.

magic output = pathname
allowable values: full Unix pathname
default: script.out

Sets the output file for the discouraged magic scripts option.
Default is the script name, followed by the extension *.out*.

magic script = pathname
allowable values: full Unix pathname
default: NULL

Sets a filename for execution via a shell whenever the file is closed
from the client, to allow clients to run commands on the server.
Use is discouraged.

mangle case = boolean
allowable values: YES, NO
default: NO

Mangles a name if it is in mixed case.

mangled map = map list
allowable values: list of to/from pairs
default: NULL

Sets up a table of names to remap (e.g., *.html* to *.htm*).

mangled names = boolean
allowable values: YES, NO
default: YES

Sets Samba to abbreviate names that are too long or have unsup-
ported characters to the DOS 8.3 style.

[global] mangled stack = number
allowable values: number
default: 50

Sets the size of the cache of recently mangled filenames.

mangling char = character
allowable values: character
default: ~

Sets the unique mangling character used in all mangled names.

---

map aliasname = pathname
allowable values: full Unix pathname
default: NULL

Points to a file of Unix group/NT group pairs, one per line. This is used to map NT aliases to Unix group names. See also the configuration options username map and map groupname.

map archive = boolean
allowable values: YES, NO
default: YES

If YES, Samba sets the executable-by-user (0100) bit on Unix files if the DOS archive attribute is set. If used, the create mask must contain the 0100 bit.

map groupname = pathname
allowable values: full Unix pathname
default: NULL

Points to a file in the format of Unix group/NT group, one pair per line. This is used to map NT group names to Unix group names. See also the configuration options username map and map aliasname.

map hidden = boolean
allowable values: YES, NO
default: NO

If YES, sets the executable-by-other (0001) bit on Unix files if the DOS hidden attribute is set. If used, the create mask option must contain the 0001 bit.

map system = boolean
allowable values: YES, NO
default: NO

If YES, Samba sets the executable-by-group (0010) bit on Unix files if the DOS system attribute is set. If used, the create mask must contain the 0010 bit.

[global] map to guest = value
allowable values: Never, Bad User, Bad Password
default: Never

If set to Bad User, allows users without accounts on the Samba system to log in and be assigned the guest account. This option can be used as part of making public shares for anyone to use. If set to Bad Password, users who mistype their passwords will be logged into the guest account instead of their own. Since no warning is given, the Bad Password value can be extremely confusing: we recommend against it. The default setting of Never prevents users without accounts from logging in.

max connections = number
allowable values: number
default: 0 (infinity)

Sets the maximum number of connections allowed to a share from each client machine.

[global] max disk size = number
allowable values: size in MB
default: 0 (unchanged)

Sets the maximum disk size/free-space size (in megabytes) to return to the client. Some clients or applications can't understand large maximum disk sizes.

[global] max log size = number
allowable values: size in KB
default: 5000

Sets the size (in kilobytes) at which Samba will start a new log file. The current log file will be renamed with an *.old* extension, replacing any previous file with that name.

[global] max mux = number
allowable values: number
default: 50

Sets the number of simultaneous operations that Samba clients may make. Avoid changing.

[global] max open files = number
allowable values: number
default: 10000

Limits the number of files a Samba process will try to keep open at one time. Samba allows you to set this to less than the Unix maximum. This option is a workaround for a separate problem. Avoid changing.

[global] max packet = number

allowable values: number in bytes
default: N/A

Obsolete as of Samba 1.7. Synonym for packet size. Use max xmit instead.

max print jobs = number

allowable values: positive integer
default: 1000

Limits the number of jobs that can be in the queue for this printer share at any one time. The printer will report "out of space" if the limit is exceeded.

[global] max ttl = number

allowable values: number of seconds
default: 14400 (4 hours)

Sets the time to keep NetBIOS names in the *nmbd* cache while trying to perform a lookup on it. Avoid changing.

[global] max wins ttl = number

allowable values: number of seconds
default: 259200 (3 days)

Limits the time-to-live, in seconds, of a NetBIOS name in the *nmbd* WINS cache. Avoid changing.

[global] max xmit = number

allowable values: size in bytes
default: 65535

Sets the maximum packet size that will be negotiated by Samba. This is a tuning parameter for slow links and older client bugs. Values less than 2048 are discouraged.

[global] message command = command

allowable values: full path to shell command
default: NULL

Sets the command to run on the server when a WinPopup message arrives from a client. The command must end in "&" to allow immediate return. Honors all % variables except %u (user), and supports the extra variables %s (filename the message is in), %t (destination machine), and %f (from).

min password length = number
allowable values: decimal number of characters
default: 5

Sets the shortest Unix password allowed by Samba when updating a user's password on its system. Also called `min passwd length`.

min print space = number
allowable values: space in KB
default: 0 (unlimited)

Sets the minimum spool space required before accepting a print request.

[global] min wins ttl = number
allowable values: number of seconds
default: 21600 (6 hours)

Sets the minimum time-to-live, in seconds, of a NetBIOS name in the *nmbd* WINS cache. Avoid changing.

name resolve order = list
allowable values: list of lmhosts, wins, hosts, bcast
default: lmhosts, wins, hosts, bcast

Sets the order of lookup when trying to get IP addresses from names. The hosts parameter carries out a regular name lookup using the server's normal sources: */etc/hosts*, DNS, NIS, or a combination of these.

[global] netbios aliases = list
allowable values: list of NetBIOS names
default: NULL

Adds additional NetBIOS names by which a Samba server will advertise itself.

netbios name = hostname
allowable values: hostname
default: varies

Sets the NetBIOS name by which a Samba server is known, or the primary name if NetBIOS aliases exist.

netbios scope = string
allowable values: string
default: NULL

Sets the NetBIOS scope string, an early predecessor of work-groups. Samba will not communicate with a machine with a different scope. This option is not recommended. It was added in 2.0.7.

[global] networkstation user login = boolean
allowable values: YES, NO
default: YES

If set to NO, clients will not do a full login when security = server. Avoid changing. Turning it off is a temporary workaround (introduced in Samba 1.9.18p3) for a Windows NT trusted domains bug. Automatic correction was introduced in Samba 1.9.18p10. The parameter may eventually be removed.

[global] nis homedir = boolean
allowable values: YES, NO
default: NO

If YES, the homedir map will be used to look up the user's home-directory server name and return it to the client. The client will contact that machine to connect to the share. This avoids mounting from a machine that doesn't actually have the disk. The machine with the home directories must be an SMB server.

[global] nt acl support = boolean
allowable values: YES, NO
default: YES

Causes the Samba server to map Unix permissions to Windows NT access control lists (ACLs). New in Version 2.0.4.

[global] nt pipe support = boolean
allowable values: YES, NO
default: YES

Allows turning off of NT-specific pipe calls. This is a developer/benchmarking option and may be removed in the future. Avoid changing.

[global] nt smb support = boolean
allowable values: YES, NO
default: YES

If YES, allows the use of NT-specific SMBs. This is a developer/
benchmarking option and may be removed in the future. Avoid
changing.

[global] null passwords = boolean
allowable values: YES, NO
default: NO

If YES, allows access to accounts that have null passwords.
Strongly discouraged.

ole locking compatibility = boolean
allowable values: YES, NO
default: YES

If YES, locking ranges will be mapped to avoid Unix locks crashing
when Windows uses locks above 32 KB. This option became obsolete in Samba 2.2.

only guest = boolean
allowable values: YES, NO
default: NO

Forces users of a share to log in as the guest account. Synonym for
guest only. Requires guest ok or public to be YES.

only user = boolean
allowable values: YES, NO
default: NO

Requires that users of the share be on a username list.

[global] oplock break wait time = number
allowable values: number
default: 10

This is an advanced tuning parameter, measured in milliseconds,
that may need to be set if a Windows system fails to release an
oplock in response to a break request from the Samba server. Due
to bugs on some Windows systems, they might fail to respond if
Samba responds too quickly; the default on this option can be
lengthened in such cases. Recommended only for experts who
know how Samba handles oplocks. New in Version 2.0.4.

---

oplock contention limit = number
allowable values: number
default: 2

This is an advanced tuning parameter and is recommended only for experts who know how Samba handles oplocks. It causes Samba to refuse to grant an oplock if the number of clients contending for a file exceeds the specified value. New in Version 2.0.4.

oplocks = boolean
allowable values: YES, NO
default: YES

If YES, supports local caching of oplocked files on the client. This option is recommended because it improves performance by about 30%. See also fake oplocks and veto oplock files.

[global] os level = number
allowable values: number
default: 0

Sets the candidacy of the server when electing a browse master. Used with the domain master or local master options. You can set a higher value than a competing operating system if you want Samba to win. Windows for Workgroups and Windows 95 use 1, Windows NT Client uses 17, and Windows NT Server uses 33.

[global] packet size = number
allowable values: number in bytes
default: 65535

Obsolete as of Samba 1.7. Synonym for max packet. Use max xmit instead.

panic action = command
allowable values: fully-qualified Unix shell command
default: NULL

Sets the command to run when Samba panics. Honors all % variables. For Samba developers and testers, /usr/bin/X11/xterm -display :0 -e gdb /samba/bin/smbd %d is a possible value.

[global] passwd chat = command sequence
allowable values: Unix server commands
default: compiled-in value

Sets the command used to change passwords on the server. Supports the variables %o (old password) and %n (new password) and allows the escapes \r \n \t and \s (space) in the sequence.

[global] passwd chat debug = boolean
allowable values: YES, NO
default: NO

Logs an entire password chat, including passwords passed, with a log level of 100. For debugging only.

[global] passwd program = program
allowable values: Unix server program
default: NULL

Sets the command used to change a user's password. Will be run as root. Supports %u (user).

[global] password level = number
allowable values: number
default: 0

Specifies the number of uppercase letter permutations used to match passwords. A workaround for clients that change passwords to a single case before sending them to the Samba server. Causes repeated login attempts with mixed-case passwords, which can trigger account lockouts.

[global] password server = netbios names
allowable values: list of NetBIOS names
default: NULL

Specifies a list of SMB servers that will validate passwords for you. Used with an NT password server (PDC or BDC) and the security = server or security = domain configuration options. Caution: an NT password server must allow logins from the Samba server.

path = pathname

allowable values: full Unix pathname
default: varies

Sets the path to the directory provided by a file share or used by a printer share. If the option is omitted, set automatically in the [homes] share to the user's home directory; otherwise defaults to */tmp*. Honors the %u (user) and %m (machine) variables.

postexec = command

allowable values: full path to shell command
default: NULL

Sets a command to run as the user after disconnecting from the share. See also the preexec, root preexec, and root postexec options.

postscript = boolean

allowable values: YES, NO
default: NO

Flags a printer as PostScript to avoid a Windows bug by inserting %! as the first line. Works only if the printer actually is PostScript compatible.

preexec = command

allowable values: full path to shell command
default: NULL

Sets a command to run as the user before connecting to the share. Synonym for exec. See also the postexec, root preexec, and root postexec options.

preexec close = boolean

allowable values: YES, NO
default: NO

If set, allows the preexec script to decide if the share may be accessed by the user. If the script returns a nonzero return code, the user will be denied permission to connect.

[global] preferred master = boolean

allowable values: YES, NO
default: NO

If YES, Samba is preferred to become the master browser. Causes Samba to call a browsing election when it comes online.

---

preload = share list
allowable values: list of shares
default: NULL

Specifies a list of shares that will always appear in browse lists. Synonym for auto services.

preserve case = boolean
allowable values: YES, NO
default: NO

If set to YES, this option leaves filenames in the case sent by the client. If NO, it forces filenames to the case specified by the default case option. See also short preserve case.

printable = boolean
allowable values: YES, NO
default: NO

Sets a share to be a print share. Required for all printers. Synonym for print ok.

[global] printcap name = pathname
allowable values: full Unix pathname
default: /etc/printcap

Sets the path to the printer capabilities file used by the [printers] share. The default value changes to */etc/qconfig* under AIX and *lpstat* on System V. Also called printcap.

print command = command
allowable values: full path to shell command
default: varies

Sets the command used to send a spooled file to the printer. Usually initialized to a default value by the printing option. This option honors the %p (printer name), %s (spool file), and %f (spool file as a relative path) variables. The command must include deletion of the spool file, or the disk will fill up.

printer = name
allowable values: printer name
default: lp

Sets the name of the Unix printer used by the share. Also called printer name.

---

printer admin = comma-separated list
allowable values: comma-separated list of usernames
default: NULL

Specifies a list of users who can administer a printer using the remote printer administration interface on a Windows system. The root user always has these privileges. New in Version 2.2.

printer driver = printer driver name
allowable values: exact printer driver string used by Windows
default: NULL

Sets the string to pass to Windows when asked what driver to use when preparing files for a printer share. Note that the value is case-sensitive.

[global] printer driver file = pathname
allowable values: full Unix pathname
default: samba-lib/printers.def

Sets the location of a *msprint.def* file, usable by Windows 95/98.

printer driver location = pathname
allowable values: Windows network path
default: *server**PRINTER$*

Sets the location of the driver for a particular printer. The value is the pathname of the share that stores the printer driver files.

printer name = name
allowable values: name
default: NULL

Synonym for printer.

printing = style
allowable values: bsd, sysv, hpux, aix, qnx, plp, lprng, caps
default: bsd

Sets the printing style to a value other than compiled-in. This sets initial values of at least print command, lpq command, and lprm command.

print ok = boolean
allowable values: YES, NO
default: NO

Synonym for printable.

[global] protocol = protocol
allowable values: NT1, LANMAN2, LANMAN1, COREPLUS, CORE
default: NT1

Sets the SMB protocol version to one of the allowable values. Resetting is highly discouraged. Only for backward compatibility with older-client bugs.

public = boolean
allowable values: YES, NO
default: NO

If YES, passwords are not needed for this share. Also called guest ok.

queuepause command = command
allowable values: full path to command
default: varies

Sets the command used to pause a print queue. Usually initialized to a default value by the printing option.

queueresume command = command
allowable values: full path to command
default: varies

Sets the command used to resume a print queue. Usually initialized to a default value by the printing option.

read bmpx = boolean
allowable values: YES, NO
default: NO

Obsolete. Do not change.

read list = comma-separated list
allowable values: comma-separated list of users
default: NULL

Specifies a list of users given read-only access to a writable share.

read only = boolean
allowable values: YES, NO
default: NO

Sets a share to read-only. Antonym of writable, writeable, and write ok.

[global] read raw = boolean
allowable values: YES, NO
default: YES

Allows fast-streaming reads over TCP using 64K buffers.
Recommended.

[global] remote announce = remote list
allowable values: list of remote addresses
default: NULL

Adds workgroups to the list on which the Samba server will
announce itself. Specified as IP address/workgroup (for instance,
192.168.220.215/SIMPLE), with multiple groups separated by
spaces. Allows directed broadcasts (i.e., ###.###.###.255). The
server will appear on those workgroups' browse lists. Does not
require WINS.

[global] remote browse sync = address list
allowable values: IP-address list
default: NULL

Enables Samba-only browse list synchronization with other Samba
local master browsers. Addresses can be specific addresses or
directed broadcasts (i.e., ###.###.###.255). The latter will cause
Samba to hunt down the local master.

[global] restrict anonymous = boolean
allowable values: YES, NO
default: NO

Denies access to users who do not supply a username. This is
disabled by default because, when the Samba server acts as the
domain's PDC, the option can keep a client from revalidating its
machine account when someone new logs in. Use of the option is
recommended only when all clients are Windows NT systems. New
in Version 2.0.4.

[global] root = pathname
allowable values: full Unix pathname
default: NULL

Synonym for root directory.

[global] root dir = pathname
allowable values: full Unix pathname
default: NULL

Synonym for root directory.

[global] root directory = pathname
allowable values: full Unix pathname
default: NULL

Specifies a directory to chroot() to before starting daemons. Prevents any access within that directory tree. See also the wide links configuration option. Also called root and root dir.

root postexec = command
allowable values: full path to shell command
default: NULL

Sets a command to run as root after disconnecting from the share. See also the preexec, postexec, and root preexec configuration options. Runs after the user's postexec command. Use with caution.

root preexec = command
allowable values: full path to shell command
default: NULL

Sets a command to run as root before connecting to the share. See also the preexec, postexec, and root postexec configuration options. Runs before the user's preexec command. Use with caution.

root preexec close = boolean
allowable values: YES, NO
default: NO

If set, allows the root preexec script to decide if the share may be accessed by the user. If the script returns a nonzero return code, the user will be denied permission to connect.

[global] security = value
allowable values: share, user, server, domain
default: user

Sets the password security policy. If security = share, services have a shared password, available to everyone. If security = user, users have (Unix) accounts and passwords. If security = server, users have accounts and passwords and a separate machine authenti-

---

cates them for Samba. If `security = domain`, full NT-domain authentication is done. See also the `password` server and `encrypted` passwords configuration options.

security mask = octal permission bits

allowable values: octal value from 0 to 0777
default: same as `create mask`

Controls which permission bits can be changed if a user on a Windows system edits the Unix permissions of files on the Samba server. Any bit that is set in the mask can be changed by the user; any bit that is clear will remain the same on the file even if the user tries to change it. Requires `nt acl support = YES`. Note that some rarely-used bits map to the DOS system, hidden, and archive bits in the file attributes in a nonintuitive way. New in Version 2.0.4.

[global] server string = string

allowable values: string
default: Samba %v

Sets the name that appears beside a server in browse lists. Honors the %v (Samba version number) and %h (hostname) variables.

set directory = boolean

allowable values: YES, NO
default: NO

Allows the DEC Pathworks client to use the *set dir* command.

[global] shared file entries = number

allowable values: number
default: 113

Obsolete; do not use.

shared mem size = number

allowable values: size in bytes
default: 102400

If compiled with FAST_SHARE_MODES (*mmap*), sets the shared memory size. Avoid changing. Became obsolete in Samba 2.2.

share modes = boolean

allowable values: YES, NO
default: YES

If set to YES, supports Windows-style whole-file (deny mode) locks.

short preserve case = boolean

allowable values: YES, NO
default: NO

If set to YES, leaves mangled 8.3-style filenames in the case sent by the client. If NO, forces the case to that specified by the default case option. See also preserve case.

[global] smb passwd file = pathname

allowable values: full Unix pathname
default: /usr/local/samba/private/smbpasswd

Overrides the compiled-in path to the password file if encrypted passwords = YES.

[global] smbrun = command

allowable values: full path to command
default: compiled-in value

Overrides the compiled-in path to the *smbrun* binary. Avoid changing.

[global] socket address = IP address

allowable values: IP address
default: NULL

Sets the address on which to listen for connections. Default is to listen to all addresses. Used to support multiple virtual interfaces on one server. Highly discouraged.

[global] socket options = list

allowable values: socket option list
default: TCP_NODELAY

Sets OS-specific socket options. SO_KEEPALIVE makes TCP check clients every four hours to see if they are still accessible. TCP_NODELAY sends even tiny packets to keep delay low. Both are recommended wherever the operating system supports them.

[global] source environment = pathname

allowable values: full Unix pathname
default: NULL

Causes Samba to read a list of environment variables from *pathname* upon startup. This can be useful when setting up Samba in a

---

clustered environment. *pathname* can begin with a "|" (pipe) character, in which case it causes Samba to run the file as a command to obtain the variables.

The file must be owned by root and must not be world-writable. If the filename begins with a "|" character, it must point to a command that is neither world-writable nor resides in a world-writable directory.

The data should be in the form of lines such as SAMBA_NETBIOS_NAME=*myhostname*. This value will then be available in the *smb.conf* files as $%SAMBA_NETBIOS_NAME. New in 2.0.7.

[global] ssl = boolean
allowable values: YES, NO
default: NO

Makes Samba use SSL for data exchange with some or all hosts. Requires Samba to be compiled with SSL support.

[global] ssl CA certDir = directory
allowable values: fully-qualified path
default: /usr/local/ssl/certs

Specifies a directory containing a file for each Certification Authority (CA) that the Samba server trusts, so that Samba can verify client certificates. Part of SSL support. Requires Samba to be compiled with SSL support.

[global] ssl CA certFile = filename
allowable values: fully-qualified path
default: /usr/local/ssl/certs/trustedCAs.pem

Specifies a file that contains information for each CA that the Samba server trusts, so that Samba can verify client certificates. Part of SSL support. Requires Samba to be compiled with SSL support.

[global] ssl ciphers = comma-separated list
allowable values: comma-separated list of ciphers
default: NULL

Specifies which ciphers should be offered during SSL negotiation. Not recommended. Requires Samba to be compiled with SSL support.

[global] ssl client cert = filename
allowable values: fully-qualified path
default: /usr/local/ssl/certs/smbclient.pem

Specifies a file containing the server's SSL certificate, for use by *smbclient* if certificates are required in this environment. Requires Samba to be compiled with SSL support.

[global] ssl client key = filename
allowable values: fully-qualified path
default: /usr/local/ssl/private/smbclient.pem

Specifies a file containing the server's private SSL key, for use by *smbclient*. Requires Samba to be compiled with SSL support.

[global] ssl compatibility = boolean
allowable values: YES, NO
default: NO

Determines whether SSLeay should be configured for bug compatibility with other SSL implementations. Not recommended. Requires Samba to be compiled with SSL support.

[global] ssl hosts = host list
allowable values: list of hosts or networks
default: NULL

Requires SSL to be used with the hosts listed. By default, if the ssl option is set, the server requires SSL with all hosts. Requires Samba to be compiled with SSL support.

[global] ssl hosts resign = host list
allowable values: list of hosts or networks
default: NULL

Suppresses the use of SSL with the hosts listed. By default, if the ssl option is set, the server requires SSL with all hosts. Requires Samba to be compiled with SSL support.

[global] ssl require clientcert = boolean
allowable values: YES, NO
default: NO

Requires clients to use certificates when SSL is in use. This option is recommended if SSL is used. Requires Samba to be compiled with SSL support.

[global] ssl require servercert = boolean
allowable values: YES, NO
default: NO

When SSL is in use, the *smbclient* requires servers to use certificates. This option is recommended if SSL is used. Requires Samba to be compiled with SSL support.

[global] ssl server cert = filename
allowable values: fully-qualified path
default: NULL

Specifies a file containing the server's SSL certificate. Requires Samba to be compiled with SSL support.

[global] ssl server key = filename
allowable values: fully-qualified path
default: NULL

Specifies a file containing the server's private SSL key. If no file is specified and SSL is in use, the server looks up its key in its server certificate. Requires Samba to be compiled with SSL support.

[global] ssl version = string
allowable values: "ssl2", "ssl3", "ssl2or3", "tls1"
default: "ssl2or3"

Defines which versions of the SSL protocol the server can use: Version 2 only ("ssl2"), Version 3 only ("ssl3"), Version 2 or 3 dynamically negotiated ("ssl2or3"), or Transport Layer Security ("tls1"). Requires Samba to be compiled with SSL support.

[global] stat cache = boolean
allowable values: YES, NO
default: YES

Makes the Samba server cache client names for faster resolution. Should not be changed.

[global] stat cache size = number
allowable values: number
default: 50

Determines the number of client names cached for faster resolution. Should not be changed.

[global] status = boolean

allowable values: YES, NO
default: YES

If set to YES, logs connections to a file (or shared memory) accessible to *smbstatus*.

strict locking = boolean

allowable values: YES, NO
default: NO

If set to YES, Samba checks locks on every access, not just on demand and at open time. Not recommended.

strict sync = boolean

allowable values: YES, NO
default: NO

If set to YES, Samba synchronizes to disk whenever the client sets the sync bit in a packet. If set to NO, Samba flushes data to disk whenever buffers fill. Defaults to NO because Windows 98 Explorer sets the bit (incorrectly) in all packets.

[global] strip dot = boolean

allowable values: YES, NO
default: NO

Removes trailing dots from filenames. Use mangled map instead.

sync always = boolean

allowable values: YES, NO
default: NO

If set to YES, Samba forces the data to disk through *fsync(3)* after every write. Avoid except to debug crashing servers.

[global] syslog = number

allowable values: number
default: 1

Sets the number of Samba log messages to send to *syslog*. Higher is more verbose. The *syslog.conf* file must have suitable logging enabled.

[global] syslog only = boolean

allowable values: YES, NO
default: NO

If set to YES, logs only to *syslog,* not standard Samba log files.

[global] time offset = number

allowable values: number of minutes
default: 0

Sets the number of minutes to add to the system time zone calculation. Provided to fix a client daylight-savings bug; not recommended.

[global] time server = boolean

allowable values: YES, NO
default: NO

If set to YES, *nmbd* provides time service to its clients.

[global] timestamp logs = boolean

allowable values: YES, NO
default: YES

Synonym for debug timestamp.

unix password sync = boolean

allowable values: YES, NO
default: NO

If set to YES, attempts to change the user's Unix password whenever the user changes his or her SMB password. Used to ease synchronization of Unix and Microsoft password databases. See also passwd chat.

unix realname = boolean

allowable values: YES, NO
default: NO

If set, provides the GCOS field of */etc/passwd* to the client as the user's full name.

update encrypted = boolean

allowable values: YES, NO
default: NO

Updates the Microsoft-format password file when a user logs in with an unencrypted password. Provided to ease conversion to encrypted passwords for Windows 95/98 and NT.

user = comma-separated list

allowable values: comma-separated list of usernames
default: NULL

Synonym for username.

username = comma-separated list

allowable values: comma-separated list of usernames
default: NULL

Sets a list of users that are tried when logging on with share-level security in effect. Also called user or users. Discouraged. Use NET USE *server**share*%*user* from the client instead.

username level = number

allowable values: number
default: 0

Specifies the number of uppercase letter permutations allowed to match Unix usernames. A workaround for the Windows feature (single-case usernames). Use is discouraged.

[global] username map = pathname

allowable values: full Unix pathname
default: NULL

Names a file of Unix-to-Windows name pairs; used to map different spellings of account names and those Windows usernames longer than eight characters.

users = comma-separated list

allowable values: comma-separated list of usernames
default: NULL

Synonym for username.

[global] utmp = boolean
allowable values: YES, NO
default: NO

This is available if Samba has been configured with the `--with-utmp` option. If set, Samba adds *utmp/utmpx* records whenever a connection is made to a Samba server. Sites can use this option to record each connection to a Samba share as a system login. New in 2.0.7.

[global] utmp consolidate = boolean
allowable values: YES, NO
default: YES

This is available if Samba has been configured with the `--with-utmp` option. Combines multiple accesses by a single user into a single login record in the *utmp* file.

[global] utmp directory = string
allowable values: full Unix pathname
default: NULL

This is available if Samba has been configured with the `--with-utmp` option. If this option and utmp are set, Samba will look in the specified directory instead of the default system directory for *utmp/utmpx* files. New in 2.0.7; also called `utmp dir`.

valid chars = list
allowable values: list of numeric values
default: NULL

Adds national characters to a character set map. Semi-obsolete; overridden by `client code page`.

valid users = user list
allowable values: list of users
default: NULL (everyone)

Specifies a list of users that can log in to a share.

veto files = slash-list
allowable values: slash-separated list of filenames
default: NULL

Specifies a list of files that the client will not see when listing a directory's contents. See also `delete veto files`.

---

veto oplock files = slash-list
allowable values: slash-separated list of filenames
default: NULL

Specifies a list of files not to oplock (and cache on clients). See also oplocks and fake oplocks.

vfs object = pathname
allowable values: full path to shared library
default: NULL

This option is used for extending Samba and is available if Samba has been configured with the --with-vfs option. It allows an additional library to be loaded, which will call for all accesses to the share. Added in 2.2.

vfs options = string
allowable values: TBD
default: NULL

Used with vfs object to pass per-share options to the library. Requires that Samba be configured with the --with-vfs option. Added in 2.2.

volume = string
allowable values: share name
default: NULL

Sets the volume label of a disk share, notably a CD-ROM.

wide links = boolean
allowable values: YES, NO
default: YES

If set, Samba follows symlinks out of the current disk share(s). See also the root dir and follow symlinks options.

[global] wins hook = command
allowable values: full path to command
default: NULL

Specifies a command to run whenever the WINS server updates its database. Allows WINS to be synchronized with DNS or other services. The command will be passed by one of the arguments add, delete, or refresh, followed by the NetBIOS name, the name

---

type (two hexadecimal digits), the time-to-live in seconds, and the IP addresses corresponding to the NetBIOS name. Requires wins service = YES.

[global] wins proxy = boolean
allowable values: YES, NO
default: NO

If set to YES, *nmbd* proxies resolution requests to WINS servers on behalf of old clients, which use broadcasts. The WINS server is typically on another subnet.

[global] wins server = hostname
allowable values: hostname
default: NULL

Sets the DNS name or IP address of the WINS server.

[global] wins support = boolean
allowable values: YES, NO
default: NO

If set to YES, Samba activates the WINS service. The wins server option must not be set if wins support = YES.

[global] workgroup = name
allowable values: workgroup name
default: compiled-in

Sets the workgroup to which things will be served. Overrides the compiled-in value. Choosing a name other than WORKGROUP is strongly recommended.

---

writable = boolean
allowable values: YES, NO
default: YES

Antonym for read only; writeable and write ok are synonyms.

---

write cache size = decimal number
allowable values: decimal number of bytes
default: 0 (disabled)

Allocates a write buffer of the specified size in which Samba accumulates data before a write to disk. This option can be used to ensure that each write has the particular size that's optimal for a

---

given filesystem. It is typically used with RAID drives, which have a preferred write size, and with systems that have a large memory and slow disks.

As of Samba 2.0.7, this option applies to the first 10 oplocked files in the shares for which it is set.

---

write list = comma-separated list
allowable values: comma-separated list of users
default: NULL (everyone)

Specifies a list of users that are given read/write access to a read-only share. See also read list.

---

write ok = boolean
allowable values: YES, NO
default: YES

Synonym for writable.

[global] write raw = boolean
allowable values: YES, NO
default: YES

Allows fast-streaming writes over TCP, using 64 KB buffers. Recommended.

[global] wtmp directory = string
allowable values: full Unix pathname
default: NULL

This is available if Samba has been configured with the --with-utmp option. If it and utmp are set, Samba looks in the specified directory instead of the default system directory for *wtmp* files. New in 2.0.7; also called wtmp dir.

Glossary of Configuration Values

Address list
    A space-separated list of IP addresses in ###.###.###.### format.

Command
    A Unix command, with a full path and parameters.

Comma-separated list
   A list of items separated by commas.

Host list
   A space-separated list of hosts. Allows IP addresses, address masks, domain names, ALL, and EXCEPT.

Interface list
   A space-separated list of interfaces, in either address/netmask or address/n-bits format. For example, 192.168.2.10/24 or 192.168.2.10/255.255.255.0.

Map list
   A space-separated list of file-remapping strings such as (*.html *.htm).

Remote list
   A space-separated list of subnet-broadcast-address/workgroup pairs. For example:

   ```
   192.168.2.255/SERVERS 192.168.4.255/STAFF
   ```

Service (share) list
   A space-separated list of share names, without the enclosing square brackets.

Slash-list
   A list of filenames, separated by "/" characters to allow embedded spaces. For example:

   ```
   /.*/fred flintstone/*.frk/
   ```

Text
   One line of text.

User list
   A space-separated list of usernames. *@group_name* includes whomever is in the NIS netgroup *group_name* if one exists, or otherwise whomever is in the Unix group *group_name*. In addition, *+group_name* is a Unix group, *&group_name* is an NIS netgroup, and &+ and +& cause an ordered search of both Unix and NIS groups.

Configuration File Variables

Table 2 lists the Samba configuration file variables.

Table 2. Variables in Alphabetic Order

Name	Meaning
%a	Client's architecture (Samba, WWfg, WinNT, Win95, or UNKNOWN)
%d	Current server process's process ID
%f	Print-spool file as a relative path (printing only)
%f	User from which a message was sent (messages only)
%G	Primary group name of %U (requested username)
%g	Primary group name of %u (actual username)
%H	Home directory of %u (actual username)
%h	Samba server's (Internet) hostname
%I	Client's IP address
%j	Print job number (printing only)
%L	Samba server's NetBIOS name (virtual servers have multiple names)
%M	Client's (Internet) hostname
%m	Client's NetBIOS name
%N	Name of the NIS home directory server (without NIS, same as %L)
%n	New password (password change only)
%o	Old password (password change only)
%P	Current share's root directory (actual)
%p	Current share's root directory (in an NIS homedir map)
%p	Print filename (printing only)
%R	Protocol level in use (CORE, COREPLUS, LANMAN1, LANMAN2, or NT1)
%S	Current share's name
%s	Name of file the message is in (messages only)
%s	Print-spool file name (printing only)
%T	Current date and time
%t	Destination machine (messages only)

Table 2. Variables in Alphabetic Order (continued)

Name	Meaning
%U	Requested username for current share
%u	Current share's username
%v	Samba version

Samba Daemons

The following sections provide information about command-line parameters for *smbd* and *nmbd*.

smbd

The *smbd* program provides Samba's file and pri services, using one TCP/IP stream and one daemon per ent. It is controlled from the default configuration *samba_dir/lib/smb.conf*, and can be overridden command-line options.

The configuration file is automatically reevaluated minute. If it has changed, most new options are imn ately effective. You can force Samba to reload configuration file immediately if you send a SIGHUP *smbd*. Reloading the configuration file, however, will affect any clients that are already connected. To escape "grandfather" configuration, a client would need to dis nect and reconnect or the server itself would have t restarted, forcing all clients to reconnect.

Other signals

To shut down an *smbd* process, send it the terminatior nal SIGTERM (–15), which allows it to die grace instead of a SIGKILL (–9). To increment the debug lo level of *smbd* at runtime, send the program a SIGUSR nal. To decrement it at runtime, send the progr SIGUSR2 signal.

Command-line options

-D

> Runs the *smbd* program as a daemon. This is the recommended way to use *smbd* (it is also the default action). In addition, *smbd* can be run from *inetd*.

-d *debug_level*

> Sets the debug (sometimes called logging) level. The level can range from 0 to 10. Specifying the value on the command line overrides the value specified in the *smb.conf* file. Debug level 0 logs only the most important messages; level 1 is normal; and levels 3 and above are primarily for debugging and slow *smbd* considerably.

-h

> Prints command-line usage information for the *smbd* program.

Testing/debugging options

-a

> If this option is specified, each new connection to the Samba server appends all logging messages to the log file. This option is the opposite of -o, and is the default.

-i *scope*

> Sets a NetBIOS scope identifier. Only machines with the same identifier will communicate with the server. The scope identifier was a predecessor to workgroups, and this option is included only for backward compatibility.

-l *log_file*

> Sends the log messages to somewhere other than the location compiled in or specified in the *smb.conf* file. The default is often */usr/local/samba/var/log.smb, /usr/samba/var/log.smb,* or */var/log/log.smb*. The first two are strongly discouraged on Linux, where */usr* may be a read-only filesystem.

-O *socket_options*

Sets the TCP/IP socket options, using the same parameters as the `socket options` configuration option. Often used for performance tuning and testing.

-o

Causes log files to be overwritten when opened (the opposite of -a). Using this option saves you from hunting for the right log entries if you are performing a series of tests and inspecting the log file each time.

-P

Forces *smbd* not to send out any network data. This option is typically used only by Samba developers.

-p *port_number*

Sets the TCP/IP port number from which the server will accept requests. Currently, all Microsoft clients send only to the default port, 139.

-s *configuration_file*

Specifies the location of the Samba configuration file. Although the file defaults to */usr/local/samba/lib/smb.conf*, you can override it here on the command line. Typically used for debugging.

nmbd

The *nmbd* program is Samba's NetBIOS name and browsing daemon. It replies to NetBIOS-over-TCP/IP (NBT) name-service requests broadcast from SMB clients, and optionally to Microsoft's Windows Internet Name Service (WINS) requests. Both are versions of the name-to-address lookup required by SMB clients. The broadcast version uses UDP/IP broadcast on the local subnet only, while WINS uses TCP/IP, which may be routed. If running as a WINS server, *nmbd* keeps a current name and address database in the file *wins.dat* in the *samba_dir/var/locks* directory.

An active *nmbd* program can also respond to browsing protocol requests used by the Windows Network Neighborhood. Browsing is a protocol that combines advertising, service announcement, and Active Directory. This protocol provides a dynamic directory of servers as well as the disks and printers that the servers are providing. As with WINS, this was initially done by making UDP/IP broadcasts on the local subnet. Now, with the concept of a local master browser, it is done by making TCP/IP connections to a server. If *nmbd* is acting as a local master browser, it stores the browsing database in the file *browse.dat* in the *samba_dir/var/locks* directory.

Signals

Like *smbd*, the *nmbd* program responds to several Unix signals. Sending *nmbd* a SIGHUP signal causes it to dump the names it knows about to the file *namelist.debug* in the *samba_dir/locks* directory and its browsing database to the *browse.dat* file in the same directory. To shut down an *nmbd* process and allow it to die gracefully, send it a SIGTERM (−15) signal instead of a SIGKILL (−9). You can increase the debug logging level of *nmbd* by sending it a SIGUSR1 signal; you can decrease it by sending a SIGUSR2 signal.

Command-line options

-D

Instructs the *nmbd* program to run as a daemon. This is the recommended way to use *nmbd*. In addition, *nmbd* can be run from *inetd*.

-d *debug_level*

Sets the debug (sometimes called logging) level. The level can range from 0 to 10. Specifying the value on the command line overrides the value specified in the *smb.conf* file. Debug level 0 logs only the most important messages; level 1 is normal; and levels 3 and above are primarily for debugging and slow *nmbd* considerably.

-h

> Prints command-line usage information for the *nmbd* program (also -?).

Testing/debugging options

-a

> If this option is specified, each new connection to the Samba server appends all logging messages to the log file. This option is the opposite of -o, and is the default.

-H *hosts_file*

> Loads a standard *hosts* file for name resolution.

-i *scope*

> Sets a NetBIOS scope identifier. Only machines with the same identifier will communicate with the server. The scope identifier was a predecessor to workgroups, and this option is included only for backward compatibility.

-l *log_file*

> Sends the log messages to somewhere other than the location compiled in or specified in the *smb.conf* file. The default is often */usr/local/samba/var/log.nmb*, */usr/samba/var/log.nmb*, or */var/log/log.nmb*. The first two are strongly discouraged on Linux, where */usr* may be a read-only filesystem.

-n *NetBIOS_name*

> Allows you to override the NetBIOS name by which the daemon will advertise itself. Specifying this option on the command line overrides the netbios name option in the Samba configuration file.

-O *socket_options*

> Sets the TCP/IP socket options, using the same parameters as the socket options configuration option. Often used for performance tuning and testing.

-o

> Causes log files to be overwritten when opened (the opposite of -a). This option saves you from hunting for

the right log entries if you are performing a series of tests and inspecting the log file each time.

-p *port_number*
Sets the UDP/IP port number from which the server will accept requests. Currently, all Microsoft clients send only to the default port, 137.

-s *configuration_file*
Specifies the location of the Samba configuration file. Although the file defaults to */usr/local/samba/lib/smb.conf*, you can override it here on the command line. Typically used for debugging.

-v
Prints the current version of Samba.

Samba Startup File

The most common way to start Samba is to run it from your Unix system's *rc* files at boot time. For systems with a System V–like set of */etc/rcN.d* directories, you can do this by placing a suitably-named script in the *rc* directory. Usually, the script starting Samba is called *S91samba*, while the script stopping or "killing" Samba is called *K91samba*. On Linux, the usual subdirectory for the scripts is */etc/rc2.d*. On Solaris, the directory is */etc/rc3.d*. For machines with */etc/rc.local* files, you would normally add the following lines to that file:

```
/usr/local/samba/bin/smbd -D
/usr/local/samba/bin/nmbd -D
```

The following example script supports two extra commands, *status* and *restart*, in addition to the normal *start* and *stop* for System V machines:

```
#!/bin/sh
#
# /etc/rc2.d./S91Samba   --manage the SMB server in a
# System V manner
#
```

```
OPTS="-D"
#DEBUG=-d3
PS="ps ax"
SAMBA_DIR=/usr/local/samba
case "$1" in
'start')
    echo "samba "
    $SAMBA_DIR/bin/smbd $OPTS $DEBUG
    $SAMBA_DIR/bin/nmbd $OPTS $DEBUG
    ;;
'stop')
    echo "Stopping samba"
    $PS | awk '/usr.local.samba.bin/ { print $1}' |\
    xargs kill
    ;;
'status')
    x=`$PS | grep -v grep | grep '$SAMBA_DIR/bin'`
    if [ ! "$x" ]; then
        echo "No samba processes running"
    else
        echo " PID TT STAT  TIME COMMAND"
        echo "$x"
    fi
    ;;
'restart')
    /etc/rc2.d/S91samba stop
    /etc/rc2.d/S91samba start
    /etc/rc2.d/S91samba status
    ;;
*)
    echo "$0: Usage error -- you must say $0 start, \
    stop, status or restart ."
    ;;
esac
exit
```

You'll need to set the actual paths and ps options to suit the machine you're using. In addition, you might want to add commands to tell Samba to reload its *smb.conf* file or dump its *nmbd* tables, depending on your actual needs.

Samba Distribution Programs

This section lists the command-line options and subcommands provided by each of the executables in the Samba distribution.

nmblookup

nmblookup is a client program that exercises the NetBIOS-over-UDP/IP name service for resolving NBT machine names into IP addresses. The program works by broadcasting its queries on the local subnet until a machine with the specified name responds. You can think of it as a Windows *nslookup(1)* or *dig(1)*. This is useful for looking up normal NetBIOS names as well as the odd ones, like _ _ MSBROWSE_ _, that the Windows name services use to provide directory-like services. If you wish to query for a particular type of NetBIOS name, add the NetBIOS <type> to the end of the name.

The command line is:

    nmblookup [options] name

The options supported are:

-A
   Interprets *name* as an IP address and does a node-status query on this address.

-B *broadcast_address*
   Sends the query to the given broadcast address. The default is to send the query to the broadcast address of the primary network interface.

-d *debug_level*
   Sets the debug (sometimes called logging) level. The level can range from 0 to 10. Debug level 0 logs only the most important messages; level 1 is normal; and levels 3 and above are primarily for debugging and slow the program considerably.

-h

Prints command-line usage information for the program.

-i *scope*

Sets a NetBIOS scope identifier. Only machines with the same identifier will communicate with the server. The scope identifier was a predecessor to workgroups, and this option is included only for backward compatibility.

-M

Searches for a local master browser. This is done through a broadcast searching for a machine that will respond to the special name _ _MSBROWSE_ _, and then asking that machine for information, instead of broadcasting the query itself.

-R

Sets the recursion desired bit in the packet. This will cause the machine that responds to try doing a WINS lookup and to return the address and any other information the WINS server has saved.

-r

Uses the root port of 137 for Windows 95 machines.

-S

Performs a node-status query once the name query has returned an IP address. This returns all the resource types that the machine knows about, with their numeric attributes. For example:

```
% nmblookup -d 4 -S elsbeth
received 6 names
        ELSBETH                 <00> - <GROUP> B <ACTIVE>
        ELSBETH                 <03> -         B <ACTIVE>
        ELSBETH                 <1d> -         B <ACTIVE>
        ELSBETH                 <1e> - <GROUP> B <ACTIVE>
        ELSBETH                 <20> -         B <ACTIVE>
        .._ _MSBROWSE_ _..      <01> - <GROUP> B <ACTIVE>
```

-s *configuration_file*

Specifies the location of the Samba configuration file. Although the file defaults to */usr/local/samba/lib/smb.conf,*

---

you can override it here on the command line. Normally used for debugging.

-T

Translates IP addresses into resolved names.

-U *unicast_address*

Performs a unicast query to the specified address. Used with -R to query WINS servers.

Note that there is no workgroup option for *nmblookup*; you can get around this by putting workgroup = *workgroup_name* in a file and passing it to *nmblookup* with the -s *configuration_file* option.

rpcclient

This is a new client that exercises the remote procedure call (RPC) interfaces of an SMB server. Like *smbclient*, *rpcclient* started its life as a test program for Samba developers and will likely stay that way for a while. Its command line is:

```
rpcclient //server/share
```

The command-line options are the same as those for the Samba 2.0 *smbclient*, and the operations you can try are listed in Table 3.

Table 3. rpcclient Commands

Command	Description
lookupsids	Resolve names from SIDs
lsaquery	Query info policy (domain member or server)
ntlogin [*username*] [*password*]	Test NT domain login
ntpass	Change NT SAM password
regcreatekey keyname [*keyvalue*]	Create registry key
regcreateval valname valtype value	Create registry value
regdeletekey keyname	Delete registry key

Table 3. rpcclient Commands (continued)

Command	Description
regdeleteval valname	Delete registry value
regenum keyname	Enumerate registry (keys, values)
reggetsec keyname	Check registry key security
regquerykey keyname	Query registry key
regtestsec keyname	Test registry key security
srvconnections	List connections on a server
srvfiles	List files on a server
srvinfo	Query server info
srvsessions	List sessions on a server
srvshares	List shares on a server
wksinfo	Query workstation info

smbclient

The *smbclient* program is the maid-of-all-work of the Samba suite. Initially intended as a testing tool, it has become a full command-line Unix client, with an FTP-like interactive client. Some of its options are still used for testing and tuning, and it is a simple tool for ensuring that Samba is running on a server.

It's convenient to look at *smbclient* as a suite of programs:

- An FTP-like interactive file transfer program
- An interactive printing program
- An interactive *tar* program
- A command-line message program
- A command-line *tar* program (but see *smbtar* later)
- A "What services do you have?" query program
- A command-line debugging program

General command-line options

The *smbclient* program has the usual set of *smbd*-like options, which apply to all the interactive and command-line use. The command-line syntax is:

```
smbclient //server_name/share_name [password]
[options]
```

The command-line options are:

-d *debug_level*
> Sets the debug (logging) level, from 0 to 10, with A for all. Overrides the value in *smb.conf.* Debug level 0 logs only the most important messages; level 1 is normal; and debug levels 3 and above are for debugging and slow *smbclient* considerably.

-h
> Prints the command-line help information (usage) for *smbclient.*

-n *NetBIOS_name*
> Allows you to override the NetBIOS name by which the program will advertise itself.

smbclient operations

Running `smbclient //server_name/share` will cause the program to prompt you for a username and password. If the login is successful, it will connect to the share and give you a prompt much like an FTP prompt (the backslash in the prompt will be replaced by the current directory within the share as you move around the filesystem):

```
smb:\>
```

From this command line, you can use several FTP-like commands, as listed in Table 4.

Table 4. smbclient Commands

Command	Description
? command	Provides a list of commands or help on a specified command.
help [*command*]	Provides a list of commands or help on a specified command.
! [*command*]	If a command is specified, runs it in a local shell. If not, places it into a local shell on the client.
dir [*filename*]	Displays any files matching *filename* in the current directory on the server, or all files if *filename* is omitted.
ls [*filename*]	Displays any files matching *filename* in the current directory on the server, or all files if *filename* is omitted.
cd [*directory*]	If *directory* is specified, changes to the specified directory on the remote server. If not, reports the current directory on the remote machine.
lcd [*directory*]	If *directory* is specified, changes the current directory on the local machine. If not, reports the name of the current directory on the local machine.
get remotefile [*localfile*]	Copies the file *remotefile* to the local machine. If *localfile* is specified, copies the file to that name. Treats the file as binary; does *not* do LF to CR/LF conversions.
put localfile [*remotefile*]	Copies *localfile* to the remote machine. If *remotefile* is specified, uses that as the name to which to copy on the remote server. Treats the file as binary; does *not* do LF to CR/LF conversions.
mget pattern	Gets all files matching *pattern* from the remote machine.
mput pattern	Places all local files matching *pattern* on the remote machine.
prompt	Toggles interactive prompting on and off for *mget* and *mput*.
lowercase ON (or OFF)	If lowercase is ON, *smbclient* converts filenames to lowercase during an *mget* or *get* (but not an *mput* or *put*).
del filename	Deletes a file on the remote machine.
md directory	Creates a directory on the remote machine.

Table 4. smbclient Commands (continued)

Command	Description
mkdir directory	Creates a directory on the remote machine.
rd directory	Removes the specified directory on the remote machine.
rmdir directory	Removes the specified directory on the remote machine.
setmode filename [+	-]rsha	Sets DOS filesystem attribute bits, using Unix-like modes. r is read-only, s is system, h is hidden, and a is archive.
exit	Exits *smbclient*.
quit	Exits *smbclient*.

There are also mask and recursive commands for large copies; see the *smbclient* man page for details on how to use these. With the exception of mask, recursive, and the lack of an ASCII transfer mode, *smbclient* works exactly the same as FTP. Note that because it does binary transfers, Windows files copied to Unix will have lines ending in carriage-return and linefeed (\r\n), not Unix's linefeed (\n).

Printing commands

The *smbclient* program can also be used for access to a printer by connecting to a print share. Once connected, the commands shown in Table 5 can be used to print.

Table 5. smbclient Printing Commands

Command	Description
print filename	Prints the file by copying it from the local machine to the remote one and then submitting it as a print job there.
*printmode text	graphics*	Instructs the server that the following files will be plain text (ASCII) or the binary graphics format that the printer requires. It's up to the user to ensure that the file is indeed the right kind.
queue	Displays the queue for the print share you're connected to, showing job ID, name, size, and status.

Finally, to print from the *smbclient*, use the -c option:

```
cat printfile | smbclient //server/printer_name \
-c "print -"
```

tar commands

smbclient can *tar* up files from a file share. This is normally done from the command line using the *smbtar* command, but the commands shown in Table 6 are also available interactively.

Table 6. smbclient Printing Commands

Command	Description
tar c	x[IXbgNa] *operands*	Performs a creation or extraction *tar* similar to the command-line program.
blocksize size	Sets the block size to be used by *tar*, in 512-byte blocks.
tarmode full	inc	reset	noreset	Makes *tar* pay attention to the DOS archive bit for all following commands. In full mode (the default), *tar* will back up everything. In inc (incremental) mode, *tar* will back up only those files with the archive bit set. In reset mode, *tar* will reset the archive bit on all files it backs up (this requires the share to be writable). In noreset mode, the archive bit will not be reset even after the file has been backed up.

Command-line message program options

-M *NetBIOS_machine_name*

Allows you to send immediate messages to another computer using the WinPopup protocol. Once a connection is established, you can type your message, pressing Ctrl-D to end. If WinPopup is not running on the receiving machine, the program returns an error.

-U *user*

Allows you to control the FROM part of the message indirectly.

Command-line tar program options

The -c (command), -D (starting directory), and -T (*tar*) options are used together to *tar* up files interactively. This is better done with *smbtar*, which we will discuss shortly. We don't recommend using *smbclient* directly as a *tar* program. Here is a list of the options and their properties:

-c *command_string*

Passes a command string to the *smbclient* command interpreter, which treats it as a semicolon-separated list of commands to be executed. This is handy for entering things such as tarmode inc, which forces smbclient -T to back up only files with the archive bit set.

-D *initial_directory*

Changes to initial directory before starting.

-T *command filename*

Runs the *tar* driver, which is *gtar* compatible. The two main commands are *c* (create) and *x* (extract), which may be followed by any of these:

a

Resets archive bits once files are saved.

b *size*

Sets the block size in 512-byte units.

g

Backs up only files with the archive bit set.

I *file*

Includes files and directories (this is the default). Does not do pattern-matching.

N *filename*

Backs up only those files newer than *filename*.

q

Suppresses diagnostics.

X *file*

Excludes files.

Command-line query program

If *smbclient* is run as:

```
smbclient -L server_name
```

it will list the shares and other services the indicated machine provides. This is handy if you don't have *smbwrappers*. It can also be helpful as a testing program in its own right.

Command-line debugging/diagnostic program options

You can use any of the various modes of operation of *smbclient* with the debugging and testing command-line options:

-B *IP_addr*
Sets the broadcast address.

-d *debug_level*
Sets the debug (sometimes called logging) level. The level can range from 0 to 10. In addition, you can specify A for all debugging options. Debug level 0 logs only the most important messages; level 1 is normal; and levels 3 and above are primarily for debugging and slow operations considerably.

-E
Sends all messages to *stderr* instead of *stdout*.

-I *IP_address*
Sets the IP address of the server to which the client connects.

-i *scope*
Sets a NetBIOS scope identifier. Only machines with the same identifier will communicate with the server. The scope identifier was a predecessor to workgroups, and this option is included only for backward compatibility.

-l *log_file*
Sends the log messages to the specified file.

-N

    Suppresses the password prompt. Unless a password is specified on the command line or this parameter is specified, the client will prompt for a password.

-n *NetBIOS_name*

    Allows you to override the NetBIOS name by which the daemon will advertise itself.

-O *socket_options*

    Sets the TCP/IP socket options using the same parameters as the socket options configuration option. Often used for performance tuning and testing.

-p *port_number*

    Sets the port number from which the client will accept requests.

-R *resolve_order*

    Sets the resolve order of the nameservers. This option is similar to the resolve order configuration option, and can take any of the four parameters, lmhosts, host, wins, and bcast, in any order.

-s *configuration_file*

    Specifies the location of the Samba configuration file. Used for debugging.

-t *terminal_code*

    Sets the terminal code for Asian languages.

-U *username*

    Sets the username and, optionally, the password (e.g., -U fred%secret).

-W *workgroup*

    Specifies the workgroup as which you would like the client to connect.

If you want to test a particular name service, run *smbclient* with -R and specify the name service. This will force *smbclient* to use only the service you indicated.

smbpasswd

The *smbpasswd* program has two distinct sets of functions, depending on who runs it. When run by ordinary users, it changes their encrypted passwords. If an ordinary user runs it with no options, *smbpasswd* connects to the primary domain controller (PDC) and changes that user's Windows password. When run by root, *smbpasswd* updates the encrypted password file.

The program will fail if *smbd* is not operating, if the hosts allow or hosts deny configuration options will not permit connections from localhost (IP address 127.0.0.1), or if the encrypted passwords option is set to NO.

Regular user options

Here is a list of regular user options:

-D *debug_level*
Sets the debug (also called logging) level. The level can range from 0 to 10. Debug level 0 logs only the most important messages; level 1 is normal; and levels 3 and above are primarily for debugging and slow the program considerably.

-h
Prints command-line usage information for the program.

-R *resolve_order*
Sets the resolve order of the nameservers. This option is similar to the resolve order configuration option, and can take any of the four parameters, lmhosts, host, wins, and bcast, in any order.

-r *remote_machine_name*
Specifies on which machine the password should change. The remote machine must be a PDC.

-U *username*
Modifies a username that is spelled differently on the remote machine. Used only with -r.

Root-only options

Here is a list of root-only options:

-a *username*
> Adds a user to the encrypted password file.

-d *username*
> Disables a user in the encrypted password file.

-e *username*
> Enables a disabled user in the encrypted password file.

-j *domain_name*
> Adds a Samba server to a Windows NT domain.

-m *machine_name*
> Changes a machine account's password. The machine accounts are used to authenticate machines when they connect to primary or backup domain controllers.

-n
> Sets no password for the user.

-s *username*
> Causes *smbpasswd* to be silent and to read its old and new passwords from standard input rather than from */dev/tty*. This is useful for writing scripts.

smbsh

The *smbsh* program lets you use a remote Windows share on your Samba server as if the share were a regular Unix directory. When you run *smbsh*, it provides an extra directory tree under */smb*. Subdirectories of */smb* are servers, and subdirectories of the servers are their individual disk and printer shares. Commands run by *smbsh* treat the */smb* filesystem as if it were local to Unix. This means that you don't need *smbmount* in your kernel to mount Windows filesystems, as you do with NFS filesystems. However, you do need to configure Samba with the --with-smbwrappers option to enable *smbsh*.

-d *debug_level*
> Sets the debug (sometimes called logging) level. The level can range from 0, the default, to 10. Debug level 0 logs only the most important messages; level 1 is normal; and levels 3 and above are primarily for debugging and slow *smbsh* considerably.

-l *logfile*
> Sets the name of the logfile to use.

-P *prefix*
> Sets the root directory on which to mount the SMB filesystem. The default is */smb*.

-R *resolve order*
> Sets the resolve order of the nameservers. This option is similar to the resolve order configuration option, and can take any of the four parameters, lmhosts, host, wins, and bcast, in any order.

-U *user*
> Supports *user%password*.

-W *workgroup*
> Sets the NetBIOS workgroup to which the client will connect.

smbstatus

The *smbstatus* program lists the current connections on a Samba server. There are three separate sections. The first section lists various shares that are in use by specific users. The second section lists the locked files that Samba currently has on all of its shares. The third section lists the amount of memory usage for each of the shares.

In the following example, lines are wrapped to fit the printed page:

```
# smbstatus
Samba Version 2.0.3
Service     uid     gid     pid     machine
```

```
--------------------------------------------------
network      davecb    davecb    7470    phoenix
(192.168.220.101) Sun May 16
network      davecb    davecb    7589    chimaera
(192.168.220.102) Sun May 16

Locked files:
Pid    DenyMode    R/W      Oplock          Name
--------------------------------------------------
7589   DENY_NONE  RDONLY   EXCLUSIVE+BATCH  /home/
samba/quicken/inet/common/system/help.bmp   Sun May 16
21:23:40 1999
7470   DENY_WRITE RDONLY   NONE             /home/
samba/word/office/findfast.exe   Sun May 16 20:51:08
1999
7589   DENY_WRITE RDONLY   EXCLUSIVE+BATCH  /home/
samba/quicken/lfbmp70n.dll   Sun May 16 21:23:39 1999
7589   DENY_WRITE RDWR     EXCLUSIVE+BATCH  /home/
samba/quicken/inet/qdata/runtime.dat   Sun May 16
21:23:41 1999
7470   DENY_WRITE RDONLY   EXCLUSIVE+BATCH  /home/
samba/word/office/osa.exe   Sun May 16 20:51:09 1999
7589   DENY_WRITE RDONLY   NONE             /home/
samba/quicken/qversion.dll   Sun May 16 21:20:33 1999
7470   DENY_WRITE RDONLY   NONE             /home/
samba/quicken/qversion.dll   Sun May 16 20:51:11 1999

Share mode memory usage (bytes):
   1043432(99%) free + 4312(0%) used + 832(0%) overhead
= 1048576(100%) total
```

smbstatus can take the following options:

-b

Forces *smbstatus* to produce brief output. This includes the version of Samba and auditing information about the users that have logged into the server.

-d

Gives verbose output, including each of the three reporting sections listed in the previous example. This is the default.

-L

> Forces *smbstatus* to print only its current file locks. This corresponds to the second section in a verbose output.

-p

> Prints only a list of *smbd* process IDs. This is often used for scripts.

-S

> Prints only a list of shares and their connections. This corresponds to the first section in a verbose output.

-s *configuration_file*
> Sets the Samba configuration file to use when processing this command.

-u *username*
> Limits the *smbstatus* report to the activity of a single user.

smbtar

The *smbtar* program is a shell script on top of *smbclient* that gives the program more intelligible options when doing *tar* operations. Functionally, it is equivalent to the Unix *tar* program.

smbtar can take the following options:

-a

> Resets the archive bit mode.

-b *blocksize*
> Sets block size. Defaults to 20.

-d *directory*
> Changes to the initial directory before restoring or backing up files.

-i

> Specifies incremental mode; *tar* files are backed up only if they have the DOS archive bit set. The archive bit is reset after each file is read.

-l *log_level*

> Sets the logging level.

-N *filename*

> Backs up only the files newer than the last modification date of *filename*. For incremental backups.

-p *password*

> Specifies the password to use to access a share.

-r

> Restores files to the share from the *tar* file.

-s *server*

> Specifies the SMB/CIFS server in which the share resides.

-t *tape*

> Specifies the tape device or file. The default is the value of the environment variable $TAPE, or *tar.out* if $TAPE isn't set.

-u *user*

> Specifies the user as which to connect to the share. You can specify the password as well, in the format *username%password*.

-v

> Specifies the use of verbose mode.

-X *file*

> Tells *smbtar* to exclude the specified file from the *tar* create or restore.

-x *share*

> States the share name on the server to which to connect. The default is backup, which is a common share name with which to perform backups.

For example, a trivial backup command to archive the data for user sue is:

```
smbtar -s pc_name -x sue -u sue -p secret -t sue.tar
```

tcpdump

The *tcpdump* utility, a classic system administration tool, dumps all the packet headers it sees on an interface that matches an expression. The version included in the Samba distribution is enhanced to understand the SMB protocol. The *expression* is a logical expression with "and," "or," and "not," although sometimes it's very simple. For example, host escrime would select every packet going to or from escrime. The expression is normally one or more of:

- host *name*
- net *network_number*
- port *number*
- src *name*
- dst *name*

The most common options are src (source), dst (destination), and port. For example, look at the following command:

```
tcpdump port not telnet
```

This command dumps all the packets except telnet. In this command, you are logged in via telnet and want to see only the SMB packets.

Another *tcpdump* example selects traffic between server and either sue or joe:

```
tcpdump host server and \( sue or joe \)
```

We recommend using the -s 1500 option so as to capture all of the SMB messages sent, instead of just the header information.

You can use many options, and many other kinds of expressions, with *tcpdump*. See Samba's man page for details on the advanced options. The most common options are as follows:

-c *count*
> Forces the program to exit after receiving the specified number of packets

-F *file*
> Reads the expression from the specified file and ignores expressions on the command line

-i *interface*
> Forces the program to listen on the specified interface

-r *file*
> Reads packets from the specified file (captured with -w)

-s *length*
> Saves the specified number of bytes of data from each packet (rather than 68 bytes)

-w *file*
> Writes the packets to the specified file

testparm

The *testparm* program checks an *smb.conf* file for obvious errors and self-consistency. Its command line is:

```
testparm [options] configfile_name [hostname IP_addr]
```

If the configuration file is not specified, the file at *<samba_dir>/lib/smb.conf* is checked by default. If you specify a hostname and an IP address, an extra check will be made to ensure that the specified machine would be allowed to connect to Samba. If a hostname is specified, an IP address should be present as well.

testparm can take the following options:

-h
> Prints command-line information for the program.

-L *server_name*

> Resets the %L configuration variable to the specified server name.

-s

> Prevents the *testparm* program from prompting the user to press the Enter key before printing a list of the configuration options for the server.

testprns

The *testprns* program checks a specified printer name against the system printer capabilities (*printcap*) file. Its command line is:

```
testprns printername [printcapname]
```

If *printcapname* isn't specified, Samba attempts to use one located in the *smb.conf* file. If one isn't specified there, Samba will try */etc/printcap*. If that fails, the program will report an error.